GREAT KNOTS
AND HOW TO TIE THEM

GREAT
KNOTS
AND HOW TO
TIE THEM

Derrick Lewis

Sterling Publishing Co., Inc. New York
A Sterling/Chapelle Book

Chapelle, Ltd.

Owner: Jo Packham
Editor: Laura Best

Staff: Marie Barber, Malissa Boatwright, Kass Burchett, Rebecca Christensen, Holly Fuller, Marilyn Goff, Michael Hannah, Shirley Heslop, Holly Hollingsworth, Susan Jorgensen, Pauline Locke, Ginger Mikkelsen, Barbara Milburn, Linda Orton, Karmen Quinney, Rhonda Rainey, Leslie Ridenour, and Cindy Stoeckl

Photographer: Kevin Dilley for Hazen Photography
Photography Styling: Susan Laws

A special thank you to Lon Elbert for sharing his knot tying skills.

Many photographs for this book were taken at the Dabb family farm in Farr West, Utah. Their hospitality is appreciated.

Library of Congress Cataloging-in-Publication Data

Lewis, Derrick
    Great knots and how to tie them / Derrick Lewis.
        p.   cm.
    "A Sterling/Chapelle book."
    Includes index.
    ISBN 0-8069-4860-4
    1. Ropework 2. Knots and splices. I. Title.
TT840.R66L49   1997
    623.88'82--dc21   97-33673
                                                        CIP

If you have any questions or comments please contact:
Chapelle, Ltd., Inc.
P.O. Box 9252
Ogden, UT 84409
(801) 621-2777
(801) 621-2788 Fax

10 9 8 7 6 5 4 3 2 1

Published by Sterling Publishing Company, Inc.
387 Park Avenue South, New York, NY 10016
©1998 by Chapelle Ltd.
Distributed in Canada by Sterling Publishing
c/o Canadian Manda Group, One Atlantic Avenue, Suite 105
Toronto, Ontario, Canada M6K 3E7
Distributed in Great Britain and Europe by Cassell PLC
Wellington House, 125 Strand
London WCR2 0BB, England
Distributed in Australia by Capricorn Link (Australia) Pty Ltd.
P.O. Box 6651, Baulkham Hills, Business Centre
NSW 2153, Australia

Printed and Bound in China
All Rights Reserved

Sterling ISBN 0-8069-4860-4

THE ART OF KNOTS

The art of knotting is as ancient as humankind. Sailors with little to do on lengthy voyages needed to find something, and with no shortage of rope or twine on board, knotting became the ideal way of passing the time. Sailors used their leisure time developing ways of tying knots that were both decorative and highly functional.

Knotting books tend to have a nautical flavor but only because so many knots have been developed on ships. Most knots, however, have been brought ashore for a number of uses.

Decorative or fancy knots and knot work have held in the past, as they do today, a particular fascination in the way they combine what is useful with the aesthetically pleasing or decorative. Their practical applications are derived from or based on well-known standard knots but they allow for individual creativity through personal ingenuity, through inventiveness, and through the complexity and precision of their formation. Knots can be as absorbing and satisfying as any puzzle. Decorative knotting has a long and distinguished history and is one of the oldest and most widely distributed of the folk arts.

There are thousands of knots, usually with more than one name, and an infinite number of variations. It is not necessary to know a great number of knots. It is more important to know a few key knots like the Sheet Bend, Bowline, Clove Hitch, and the Figure Eight and learn to tie them correctly and quickly. The only way to gain the necessary confidence is to practice knots over and over again until the movements become automatic and instinctive.

TABLE OF

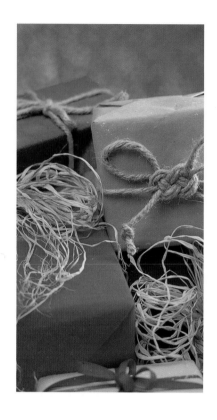

CONTENTS

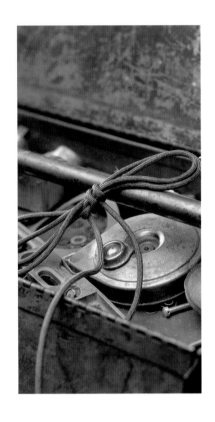

GENERAL INFORMATION

The main factor to consider when selecting one knot above another is the strength. Other factors influencing choice are the speed and ease with which a knot can be tied, the size of the finished knot, and the knot's reliability. Select the right knot for the right job. Remember: knots perform differently under different sorts of strain; knots that hold under some conditions will slip under others. This basic principle of rope work is one of the most intriguing aspects of this art form. All manipulations with a rope fall into three general classifications: knots, hitches, and bends.

KNOT

A knot is a tie made in a rope which requires manipulation of only one end. Both ends may be used when the rope is short enough.

HITCH

A hitch is used primarily for attaching a rope to another object.

BEND

A bend involves joining two ropes together so they will stand the strain of being used as one long rope.

PARTS OF A KNOT

GLOSSARY

Bend: The action of tying two ropes together by their ends.

Bight: Slack section of rope between working end and standing end.

Braid: To interweave several strands.

Carabiner: A metal snap link used by climbers as an attachment.

Chafe: To make or become worn or frayed by rubbing.

Cord: Several tightly twisted yarns making a line.

Double: To follow lead strand of a decorative knot an additional time.

Dropper: Short length of line, with a wet fly attached, joined onto the leader between the line and end fly.

End: The end of the length of rope that is being knotted.

Eye: A seized loop formed at the end of a length of rope.

Fray: To unravel, especially the end of a piece of rope.

Frog: A decorative button closure.

Guy: Any rope used for steadying purposes.

Halyard: Rope for hoisting flags, sails, and similar objects.

Hawser: A large rope used for towing or mooring.

Heaving Line: A line with a weighted knot tied at one end, attached to another heavier line which is thrown from boat to shore or to another vessel.

Hitch: Knot made to secure a rope to a post, ring, spar, or to another rope.

Lanyard: A short length of rope made decorative with knots, used to secure objects.

Lash: Secure by binding with rope.

Lay: The twist pattern of a three strand rope.

Lead: The direction the working end takes through a knot.

Leader: Thin, tapering length of nylon that forms a connection between a fly line and a fly.

Line: A general label for most cordage with no specific purpose, although it can describe a particular use.

Loop: Part of rope which is bent so that it crosses itself.

Marline: Cordage used for seizing or whipping a large rope.

Marlingspike: A pointed instrument, usually of iron, used to separate the strands of rope.

Middle: Finding the center of the rope by laying two ends together.

Over-and-Under: Description of the weave in knots.

Rope: Strong, thick cord made from twisted strands of fiber or wire.

Seized: Bind end of rope with small stuff to prevent unraveling.

Slack: Part of rope that is not under tension.

Small Stuff: Thin twine, string, rope, or line.

Spar: Any pole supporting a ship's sail.

Splice: Join ends of rope by interweaving strands.

Stage: A plank of timber, when suspended as a working platform.

Standing End: End of standing part of rope.

Standing Part: Main, non-working part of a line.

Stopper Knot: Used to bind end of a line, cord, or rope to prevent unraveling or provide a decorative end.

Strand: Yarns twisted together to make rope.

Strop: Rope or strap seized around a pulley block to suspend it.

Taut: Tightly stretched.

Turn: When the working end is passed around the standing part.

Whipping: A series of turns of small stuff at end of rope to prevent fraying.

Work: To draw up and shape a knot.

Working End: Part of the rope used actively in tying a knot.

TIE IT SIMPLE

Square Knot

BASIC KNOTS

OVERHAND KNOT • HALF KNOT • OVER-AND-UNDER • SIMPLE TWIST • SINGLE KNOT • THUMB KNOT

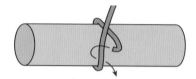

1. Make a loop in standing part of rope. Bring end through loop.

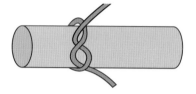

The Overhand Knot is perhaps the easiest and most well-known knot.

2. Pull both ends to tighten. Completed Overhand Knot.

SLIP KNOT • NOOSE • RUNNING KNOT • SINGLE BOW

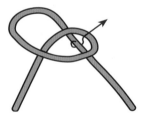

1. Make an Overhand Knot, leaving one end long. Fold longer end into a bight and insert into turn.

The Slip Knot is made in small-diameter rope to tie packages or snare birds and rabbits.

2. When tightened, the knot holds the bight. Completed Slip Knot.

SQUARE KNOT • COMMON KNOT • FLAT KNOT
• HARD KNOT • REEF KNOT • REGULAR KNOT
• STRING TIE KNOT • TRUE KNOT

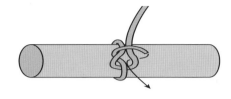

1. Make an Overhand Knot.

The Square Knot is used to tie ropes of equal thickness together. It is popular because it is easy to tie and untie, yet holds firmly.

2. Make an Underhand Knot. Completed Square Knot.

COLLECTION KNOT

A Collection Knot is an Overhand Knot made up of several strands to form a fringe or tassel.

FROST KNOT

A Frost Knot is an Overhand Knot tied in webbing, which may be used as an improvised ladder.

GRANNY KNOT • CALF KNOT • FALSE KNOT
• GARDEN KNOT • GRANARY KNOT • LUBBER'S KNOT

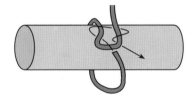

1. Make two Overhand Knots.

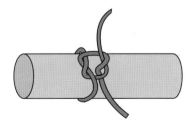

The Granny Knot is a mistake form of the Square Knot which fails to pull flat. It is easy to untie and is often used on grain sacks.

2. Completed Granny Knot.

13

HALF HITCH

A Half Hitch is usually the first step in making other hitches. It is also added at the end of a hitch for extra security or used as a temporary knot.

1. Pass rope through ring. Go behind standing part into loop eye. Completed Half Hitch.

SLIPPED HALF HITCH
- CANOE HITCH
- SLIPPERY HITCH

This variation of the Half Hitch, is easy to cast off when the rope is under strain.

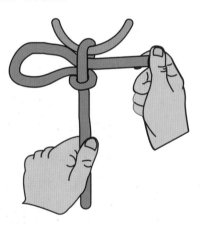

1. Make a Half Hitch. Take end back through loop creating a bight. Completed Slipped Half Hitch.

SINGLE HITCH

The Single Hitch is a Half Hitch tied around its standing part instead of tied around an object.

SEIZED HALF HITCH

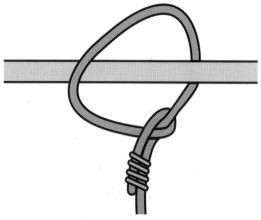

A Seized Half Hitch will hold a permanent circular shape.

1. Make a Half Hitch. Holding ends together, lash small stuff around ends to secure. Completed Seized Half Hitch.

COW HITCH • BALE SLING HITCH • CARRIAGE HITCH • DEAD EYE HITCH • GIRTH HITCH • HOIST HITCH • LANYARD HITCH • LARK'S HEAD • RING HITCH • RUNNING EYE • SLING HITCH • TAG LOOP

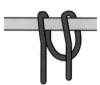

1. Take a bight in center of rope and encircle object.

2. Bring ends through bight.

From macrame to climbing, this versatile hitch is easy to tie and release.

3. Pull ends tight. Completed Cow Hitch.

CLOVE HITCH • BOATMANS' KNOT • BUILDERS' KNOT
• DOUBLE HALF HITCH • PEG KNOT • STEAMBOAT HITCH

The Clove Hitch is used to tie a rope to a stationary object, to secure a boat, or to make lashes. It is simple to untie, and will not jam under strain.

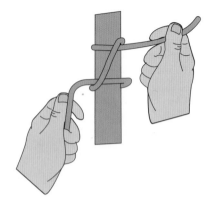

2. Push loops close together.

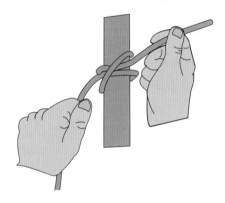

3. Pull tight. Completed Clove Hitch.

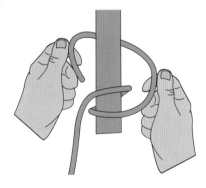

1. Bring free end around pole counterclockwise. Lay line over standing part. Bring end once more around pole. Insert under diagonal loop.

SCAFFOLD HITCH

Two Clove Hitches run together make a safe hitch to hold a scaffold.

OKLAHOMA HITCH

Pulling the two parts of a Clove Hitch in opposite directions results in an Oklahoma Hitch. This increases the friction grip when stretching a rope fence along a series of posts.

TAUT-LINE HITCH

This modification of the Clove Hitch forms a loop that will not slip when rope is tight. It is useful for tightening a clothesline or as guy ropes for a tent. It is easy to tie and untie.

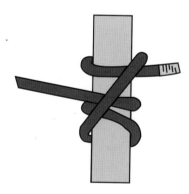

1. Pass rope through a ring or around a peg. Carry free rope end counterclockwise and down standing part twice. Come up through loop formed. Tighten around standing part. Completed Taut-Line Hitch.

CONSTRICTOR KNOT

The Constrictor Knot is used to seize bundles of loose material, or for closing necks of bags. The knot is simple to tie yet possesses a ratchet-like bulldog grip. It is not meant to be untied.

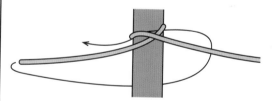

1. Take two turns around object. Make an Overhand Knot (pg 12).

2. Thread left end under first turn, trapping Overhand Knot. Completed Constrictor Knot.

PARCEL KNOT

This variation of the Constrictor Knot (pg 17) adds a bight as the final step allowing the knot to be untied easily.

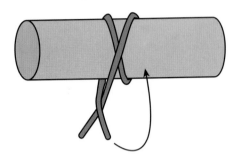

1. Take two turns around object. Make an Overhand Knot (pg 12).

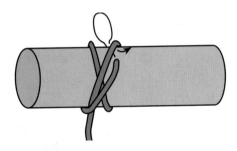

2. Thread left end under first turn, trapping Overhand Knot.

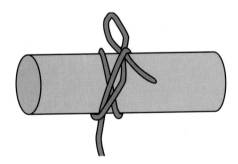

3. Bring the end back through loop forming a bight. Completed Parcel Knot.

MILLER'S KNOT

This variation of the Constrictor Knot (pg 17) is often suggested in farm bulletins to secure grain bags. Like the Constrictor Knot, it is not meant to be untied.

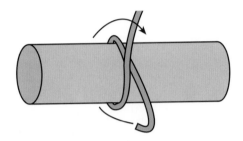

1. Wrap rope around object, crossing rope in front.

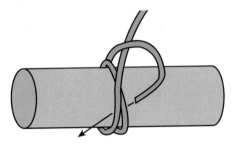

2. Bring end under both wrapped ropes.

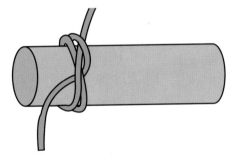

3. Pull tight. Completed Miller's Knot.

TRANSOM KNOT

Similar to the Constrictor Knot, this knot is used to secure paddles to canoes, skis and bicycles to luggage racks, and for tying up bean poles. It can be undone but it is often simpler to cut through cord diagonally.

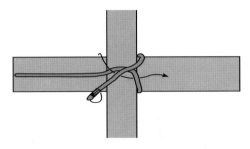

1. Loop cord around horizontal pole. Cross over end in front.

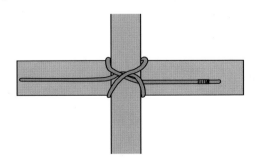

2. Wrap end around vertical pole. Weave end under cord. Pull tight. Completed Transom Knot.

STRANGLE KNOT

When tied around a single object, the Transom Knot becomes the Strangle Knot. To make the Strangle Knot temporary, form a bight in one end.

ROLLING HITCH

The Rolling Hitch is commonly used to hoist light tools, pipes, and long objects.

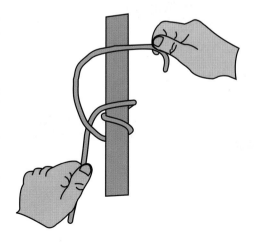

1. Loop line around pole twice.

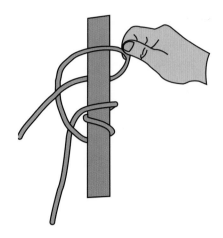

2. Make a Half Hitch on top.

3. Pull tight. Completed Rolling Hitch.

STEEPLEJACK HITCH
• SAFETY-BELT HITCH

This modification of the Rolling Hitch is used to climb steeples or tall buildings.

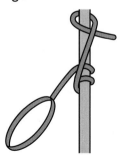

1. Loop line around spar twice. Add an extra half turn. Completed Steeplejack Hitch.

SLACK LINE HITCH

The Slack Line Hitch will hold well when tied to either a slack rope or cable. When snugly drawn, it can be pulled from either direction.

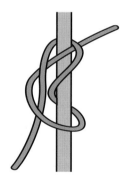

1. Take rope around cable or spar. Wrap one end back to front. Secure under original bight.

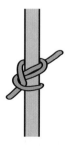

2. Completed Slack Line Hitch.

SHEET BEND • BECKET BEND • COMMON BEND
• FLAG BEND • ORDINARY BEND • SIMPLE HITCH
• SWAB HITCH

The Sheet Bend joins two lines without slipping or coming untied. This bend can withstand a great deal of strain and is easy to undo.

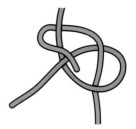

2. Twist smaller rope over and under loop.

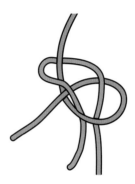

3. Bring small rope back over loop and under itself.

4. Pull standing parts of both ropes sideways to tighten knot. Completed Sheet Bend.

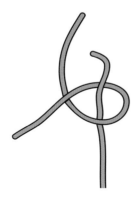

1. Form a bight in the heavier rope. Bring small rope end through loop.

WEAVER'S KNOT

The Weaver's Knot is a Sheet Bend tied in yarn or twine to join threads that come apart.

21

DOUBLE SHEET BEND

The Double Sheet Bend is a secure bend because two or more turns are added around the heavier rope.

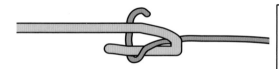

1. Make a loop with end of heavy rope.

2. Weave end of small rope through loop.

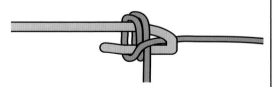

3. Wrap small rope around one more time. Pull tight. Completed Double Sheet Bend.

SLIPPED SHEET BEND

When the Sheet Bend is slipped it is easier to untie when rope is under heavy strain.

1. Tie a Double Sheet Bend but slip the end instead of pulling through the last loop of the lighter rope.

2. Completed Slipped Sheet Bend.

HONDA KNOT
• BOWSTRING KNOT

The Honda Knot is often confused with a Lariat but it is actually just the first step in making a Lariat. Though simple, this knot must be carefully formed, so when it is drawn tight the stopper knot will catch and hold.

1. Tie an Overhand Knot (pg 12) in rope end to serve as a stopper.

2. Tie a loose Overhand Knot in standing part, above end. Let end emerge from front of loop to right.

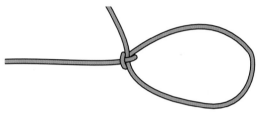

3. Bring end in back of loop and draw up through from left. Form a loop within loop with end going through lower portion of knot. Completed Honda Knot.

LARIAT • LASSO NOOSE

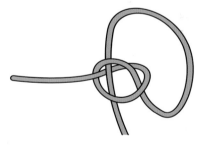

1. Make a Honda Knot. Draw a bight through large loop to form a running noose.

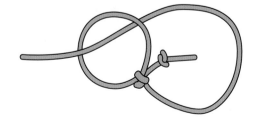

2. Completed Lariat.

23

Bow Knot
Shoelace Special

BOW KNOT

- DOUBLE-SLIPPED REEF
- SHOESTRING KNOT

Simple and widely used, this knot can be undone quickly.

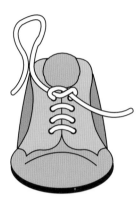

1. Make an Overhand Knot (pg 12). Take a bight in the standing part.

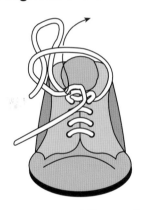

2. Tie working end around bight forming second knot.

3. Pull loop through. Be certain loops are equal. Completed Bow Knot.

SHOELACE SPECIAL

This variation of the Bow Knot is an effective way of keeping shoestrings tight. It takes longer to undo both knots, but they stay tied while in use.

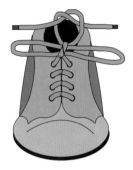

1. Make an Overhand Knot (pg 12) on top of Bow Knot.

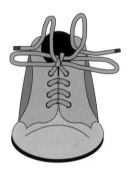

2. Tie another Bow Knot on top of first Bow Knot.

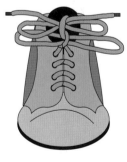

3. Tighten and center both Bow Knots. Completed Shoelace Special.

HANGMAN'S NOOSE • JACK KETCH'S KNOT

This strong noose slides easily without coming undone and withstands sudden jerks.

2. Tighten turns one at a time. Finish at eye of second loop.

3. Pull eye of knot and slide turns left. Check that noose runs freely. Completed Hangman's Noose.

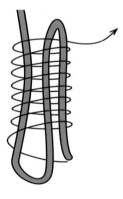

1. Make loop desired size, leaving a long end. Wrap working end seven times from right to left. Bring end through top loop and pull bottom loop tight.

PARADE LOOP

A Hangman's Noose made in white cord and displayed by calvary horses on review is called the Parade Loop.

STOPPER KNOTS

INTERMEDIATE STOPPER KNOT

1. Make a figure eight.

2. Bring end through top loop.

This stopper knot can aid in removing a floating cork from a bottle. Pour contents into a clean receptacle. Tie stopper in end of strong string. Push knotted end into bottle reaching just below beginning of bottle neck. Tilt bottle allowing cork to slide down neck toward mouth. Gently pull string up into neck catching cork at its lower end. With an easy pull on the string, the cork will be pulled out of the bottle. Pour liquid back and apply new cork.

3. Pull tight. Completed Intermediate Stopper Knot.

OYSTERMAN'S STOPPER

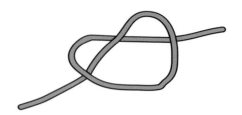

1. Make an Overhand Knot (pg 12).

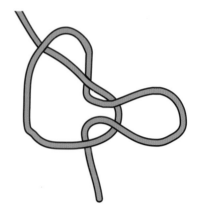

2. Bring rope underneath forming a bight.

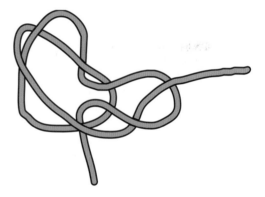

3. Bring end around and up through bight.

4. Pull tight. Completed Oysterman's Stopper.

This stopper is used to form a large stopper knot in heavy rope.

28

QUATREFOIL

This modification of the Oysterman's Stopper is used in medium sized rope.

1. Make a loop.

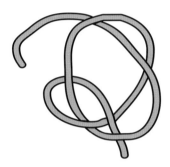

2. Bring end through loop and then through newly formed loop.

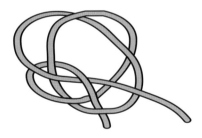

3. Weave end back through original loop and over other two lines.

4. Pull tight. Completed Quatrefoil.

STEVEDORE KNOT

This stopper knot is used to prevent the rope end from passing through a cargo block or eyebolt.

1. Loop end over standing part. Bring end through original loop.

2. Pull tight. Completed Stevedore Knot. A toggle may be inserted to make knot easier to untie.

PACKAGES

BAG KNOT • CROSSING HITCH

The Bag Knot locks crossing points on bottom of parcels.

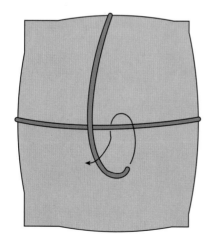

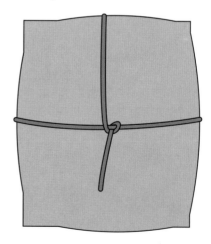

1. Take string around front of package vertically. Turn package 45 degrees twisting string to face other direction. Bring end over and under stationary piece.

2. Pull ends tight. Completed Bag Knot. Secure rest of package on top with a Package Knot or Packer's Knot.

PACKER'S KNOT

- ## FIGURE EIGHT SLIP KNOT

The Packer's Knot is an easily tied knot used for securing meat packages or for holding wrapping on parcels.

1. Make a figure eight around standing part, forming a running loop. Place loop around package and pull tight.

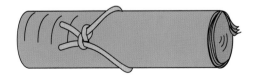

2. Completed Packer's Knot.

PACKING KNOT

The Packing Knot is a variation on the Packer's Knot. After cinching the knot next to the package this knot can be secured with Half Hitches (pg 14).

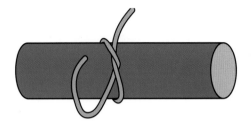

1. Make an Overhand Knot (pg 12) around the object to be secured.

2. Bring left end around right.

3. Make a Half Hitch (pg 14) with the right end.

4. Pull tight. Completed Packing Knot.

31

FLORIST'S KNOT

Though this knot is formed with a Slip Knot, the knot holds tight while still retaining a loop for decorative purposes.

1. Make an Overhand Knot (pg 12) around package. Form a Slip Knot (pg 12) on top of Overhand Knot.

2. Make a Half Hitch (pg 14) around loop formed by Slip Knot. Pull tight to prevent slippage. Completed Florist's Knot.

PACKAGE KNOT

The Package Knot is actually made of a combination of knots. The combination of a Bowline and Half Hitches not only seals the box shut for mailing, it also provides a handle for carrying on a plane or trip.

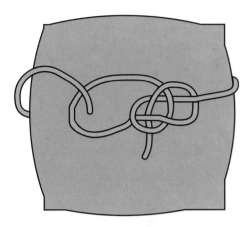

1. **Wrap cord horizonally around package. Tie a Bowline (pg 83-84) and bring end through Bowline.**

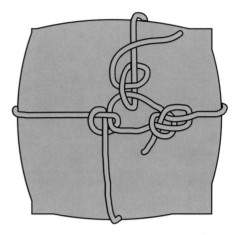

3. **Bring end through loop in center of package. Make two Half Hitches (pg 14) over standing end.**

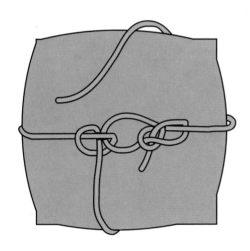

2. **Secure end through Bowline with an Overhand Knot (pg 12). Wrap cord vertically around package.**

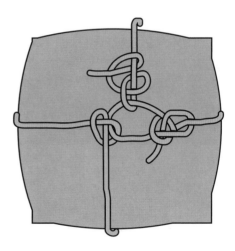

4. **Tighten as needed. Completed Package Knot.**

TIES

BOW TIE

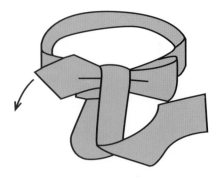

2. Make a bow on left side. Swing inside, over first bow's lead, and make a bow to the right.

3. Pull the right bow through. Shape but not too well. Completed Bow Tie.

Though tied differently, this Bow Tie is much like the Bow Knot.

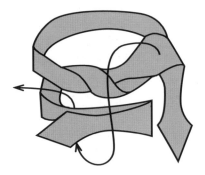

1. Make an Overhand Knot (pg 12). Bring right half over then under left. The outside half is longer.

COVENTRY BOW

This is a different way to tie a Bow Tie for the neck.

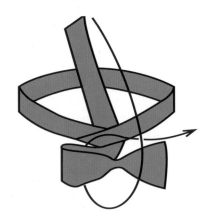

1. Fold tie into a loop and bring other end over top.

**2. Secure loose end in back.
Completed Coventry Bow.**

BUNTLINE HITCH
• CRAVAT

**1. Cross wide end over narrow.
Twist around tie, bring back to
front. Bring wide end down
through twisted loop.**

Historically the Buntline Hitch was
used on the eyes of sails as an aid
to furling them. The short end inside
would jam the rope in a strong wind.
When made in flat material, it is the
knot often found in a necktie.

**2. Pull tight by adjusting top knot
and pulling down on narrow end.
Completed Buntline Hitch.**

FOUR IN HAND

The Four in Hand resembles the Buntline Hitch but is tied differently.

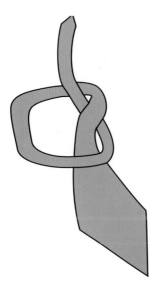

3. Push short end in. Completed Four in Hand.

1. The left end slips under the right, then makes two round turns. The end comes up through the crossing from behind and down through last turn.

2. Shape tie knot. Tuck through tie keeper.

HALF WINDSOR

This necktie knot is best worn with an elegant shirt and a silk tie.

1. Wrap wide end around narrow end.

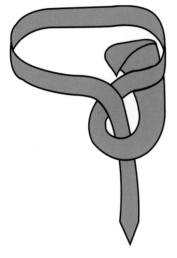

2. Bring wide end behind and over.

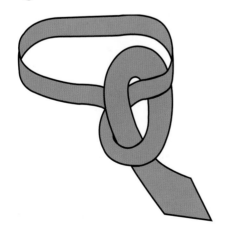

3. Bring wide end through loop.

4. Pull wide end tight. Adjust knot to neck. Completed Half Windsor.

WINDSOR
• DOUBLE WINDSOR

The Windsor makes a more uniform knot than the Half Windsor because it takes a loop from both sides.

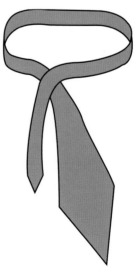

1. Wrap narrow end around wide.

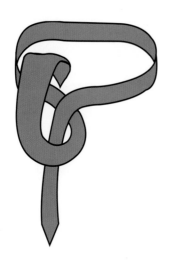

2. Bring wide end over narrow.

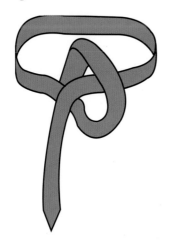

3. Pull down from behind.

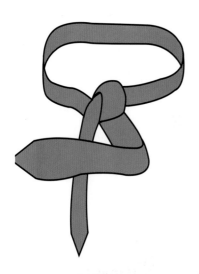

4. Bring wide end to front and cross over narrow end.

5. Bring wide end up from behind again to form a Windsor.

6. Pull wide end through.

7. Even out knot at neck. Completed Windsor.

TIE IT FANCY

Chinese Button Knot

BOWS

JAPANESE PARCEL
• GIFT KNOT

2. Form a bight on other side and weave through center.

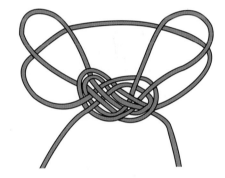

3. Pull up on ears and down on ends to tighten. Completed Japanese Parcel.

This attractive knot, tied in double ends, is based on the symmetrical Carrick Bend (pg 99). It is ideal for gift tying. If tied in ribbon, ends can be cut or trimmed into a diagonal or swallowtail shape. If tied in cord, ends can be finished off with an Overhand Knot (pg 12).

1. Make a bight in center of ribbon. Bring bight over to form loop.

FOUR-LOOP CROWN

This decorative parcel or gift knot is created by crowning four loops.

1. Arrange cord in loops.

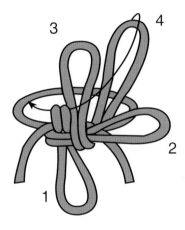

2. Crown loop 1 by bringing it to right of loop 2. Cross loop 2 to right and crown with loop 3.

3. Crown loop 3 with loop 4 and tuck under the double bight created by loop 1. Arrange all parts of knot to give an equal appearance. Tighten. Completed Four-Loop Crown.

SHAMROCK KNOT

This knot is made in leather, cording, wire for jewelry, or tied on a gift.

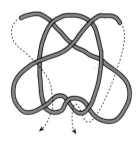

1. Tie an Overhand Knot (pg 12). Carry right end toward left. Lay left end across loop. Carry end down over both portions of bight.

2. Bring ends around side loops.

3. Pull ends down, tightening center and at same time arranging three big loops. Completed Shamrock Knot.

FLOWER KNOT

This variation of the Shamrock Knot is used as jewelry or as a fastener.

1. Tie a Shamrock Knot (pg 41-42). Make top loop twice as large as others. Bring top loop down under two horizontal cords in knot center.

2. Top loop is at bottom, forming lower petal. The two loops at top form a five-petaled flower. Completed Flower Knot.

TRUE LOVER'S LOOP
- CROSS KNOT
- SOUTHERN CROSS KNOT
- TWO-STRAND LANYARD

This variation of the Shamrock Knot is used as decoration on bags and purses.

1. Make a Shamrock Knot (pg 41-42). Pull loops tight forming a knot. Completed True Lover's Loop.

SCARVES

DECORATIVE SQUARE KNOT • JAPANESE BEND

This knot should not be confused with the Reef Knot or Square Knot. The Decorative Square Knot is used to tie a scarf or sash with ends lying perfectly. A knotted scarf can be displayed in front, to the side, or in back.

1. Loop right end of scarf over left. Take left end around and over right.

3. Tighten knot evenly.

2. Bring left end through newly formed bight.

4. The front looks like a square, the back a cross. Completed Decorative Square Knot.

TRIANGULAR DRAPE

This decorative knot ties a long scarf to be worn with one scarf end flowing down the back.

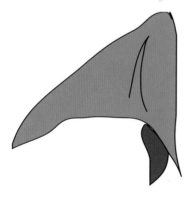

1. Fold square into triangle.

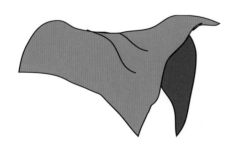

2. Place triangle point over right shoulder. Toss front end in front of neck and over left shoulder. Let it drop down the back.

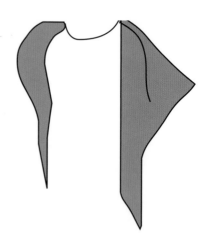

3. Take left end from behind neck, wrap over right end from top.

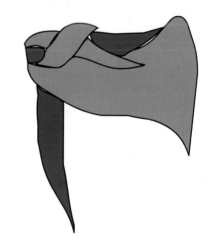

4. Knot around itself.

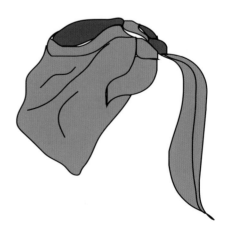

5. Arrange scarf so tail hangs down back and triangular piece is at front of neck. Completed Triangular Drape.

ROSETTE

The Rosette is commonly worn around the neck or at the waist.

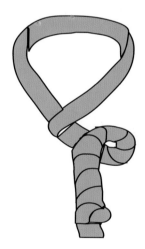

1. Wrap scarf around neck or waist, bring ends to front. Twist ends together forming a tight coil.

2. Make an Overhand Knot (pg 12) in coiled scarf.

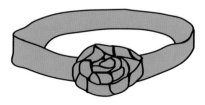

3. Wrap twisted ends into a continuous circle. Pull end tips through center of circle from back of rosette. Completed Rosette.

BUTTONS

Square Button Knot
Caterpillar Knot

SQUARE BUTTON KNOT

This decorative button can be used with the Caterpillar Knot or a frog.

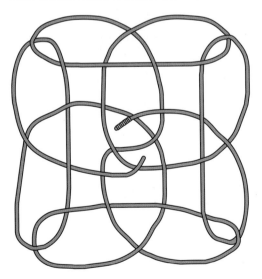

1. Lay cord on flat surface. Starting with marked end, make two overlapping loops on the right, top, bottom, then left. Bring end back to the center.

2. Carefully work knot bringing each turn in evenly. It may help to use a pin to manipulate the cords once they begin to tighten. Completed Square Button Knot.

CATERPILLAR KNOT

The Caterpillar Knot can be decorative alone or used as a fastening on clothing. The knot can be made as long or short as desired depending on the number of loops formed.

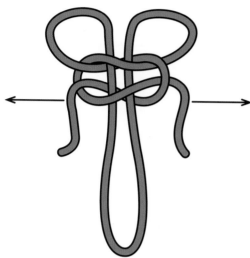

1. Make a bight in cord center. Loop ends. Make an Overhand Knot (pg 12) through loops.

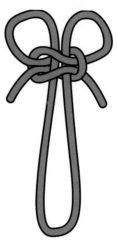

3. Repeat until desired number of loops are tied.

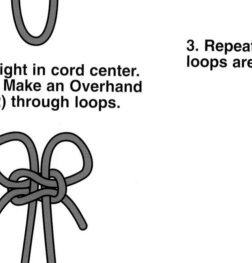

2. Pull ends to tighten.

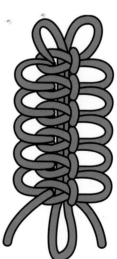

4. Completed Caterpillar Knot.

Napoleon's Knot
Circular Flat Top Knot

NAPOLEON'S KNOT

This decorative knot can be used as an accent or as a button clasp.

1. Make an Overhand Knot (pg 12).

2. Form loop in front of Overhand Knot.

3. Bring end through loop.

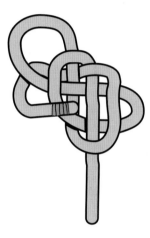

4. Weave around center end. Weave through center.

5. Tighten as desired. Completed Napoleon's Knot.

CIRCULAR FLAT TOP KNOT

This decorative button can be used with Napoleon's Knot or a frog.

1. **Make three large loops next to one another. In center, change position and make three large loops the opposite direction. Bring both ends together in center of knot. Work knot carefully until all loops are pulled in equally.**

2. Completed Circular Flat Top Knot.

ORIENTAL KNOT

1. Form a loop in center of cord and form two others on each side. Make one overhand, the other underhand. Cross line ends right over left up through lower loops.

2. Weave ends up through top loop. Left going under loop, over right end, and under loop; right going over loop, under left end and over loop.

3. Completed Oriental Knot.

Typical of many knots of Oriental origin, this knot is formed by weaving line through loops.

PENTAGON

This decorative knot can be worn as an accent or a button clasp.

1. Make two large loops next to one another in a counter-clockwise direction. In center change position and make two large loops the opposite direction. Bring both ends together in center of knot. Work knot carefully until all loops are pulled in equally.

2. Completed Pentagon.

CASKET KNOT

This decorative knot can be worn as an accent or a button clasp.

1. Make two large loops next to one another in a counter-clockwise direction. In center change position and make two large loops the opposite direction. Bring both ends together in center of knot. Work knot carefully until all loops are pulled in equally.

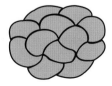

2. Completed Casket Knot.

CHINESE BUTTON KNOT • PAJAMA KNOT

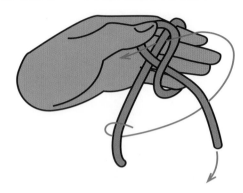

2. Weave left and right ends through middle forming four intertwined loops.

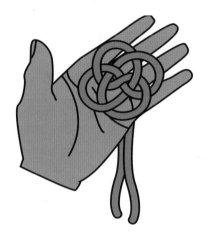

This knot is worn throughout China on underwear and night-clothes, as a fastener, replacing buttons of wood or bone.

3. This button can be left loose by seizing the back to keep its shape or can be worked into a tight button as in Step 4.

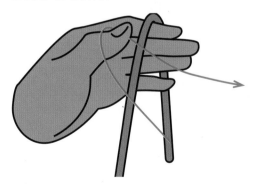

4. Carefully work knot until end is tight and uniform. Completed Chinese Button Knot.

1. Drape rope over hand. Bring back end around outside thumb. Take front end between rope and fingers. Take back rope behind front and under itself in loop.

PULLS

COMMERCIAL CURTAIN CORD KNOT

This decorative knot can be used to shorten curtain cords or other decorative lines.

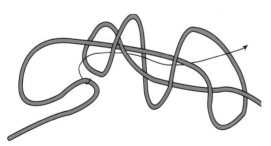

1. Loop end around standing part.

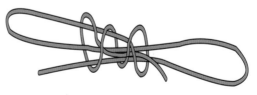

2. Pull ends to tighten around loops.

3. Pull tight. Completed Commercial Curtain Cord Knot.

Capuchin Knot

CAPUCHIN KNOT • FANCY BLOOD KNOT
• MULTIPLE OVERHAND

This knot is used by Capuchin monks on the end of their belt cords. The art of tying this knot is to make the loop disappear into the knot.

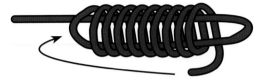

1. Make a small bight near end of cord. Make three to nine turns around standing part. Bring through turns. Pull standing part and end to tighten.

2. Make bight merge with turns.

3. Completed Capuchin Knot.

FOUR-PLY KNOT

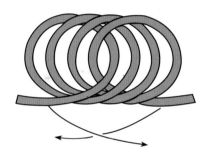

1. Coil rope around into four intertwined circles. Cross ends, bringing circles together.

2. Pull ends to tighten.

This knot can be deceptively difficult to tie if instructions are not followed exactly.

3. Work knot until tight and curves are uniform. Completed Four-Ply Knot.

CHINESE LOOP

The Chinese Loop is decorative, but secure.

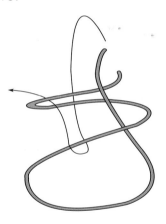

1. Form a bight and a loop. Bring end over bight. Weave end through bight.

2. Pull end to tighten. Completed Chinese Loop.

TWO HEARTS BEAT AS ONE

This decorative knot can be used to shorten a rope.

1. Loop rope four times intertwining with next loop.

2. Weave center loop to outside. Pull tight, sliding knot into the middle.

3. Completed Two Hearts Beat as One.

MONKEY'S FIST • BUTTON KNOT
• HEAVING LINE KNOT • POUCH KNOT

2. Wind another three times around middle.

This decorative knot has many practical uses, the most common being at the end of a "heaving line" to be thrown from boat to shore or to another vessel. The purpose of the heaving line is to draw behind it a heavier line or rope to use for tying up. It can be made at the end or in the middle of a rope. It is used to cover any small round objects, from paper-weights to cane heads and door handles. It is regularly used at the end of pull cords.

3. Wind a third three times up through loops of original ball.

5. Work knot by tightening the nine turns individually. Completed Monkey's Fist.

4. Wrap three times in center.

JAPANESE LOOP

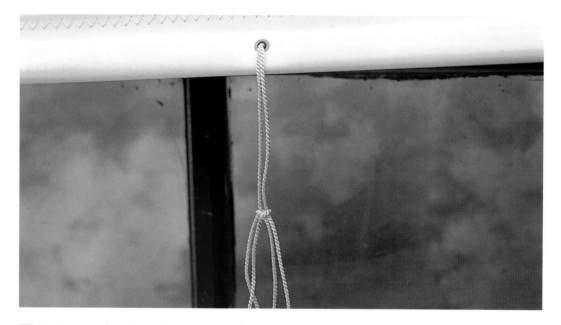

This decorative knot is used to decorate the end of a cord such as a window shade or light pull.

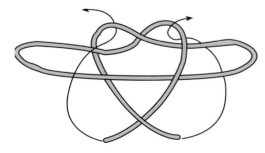

1. Make an Overhand Knot (pg 12). Bring loops through both sides. Take ends up through top loops.

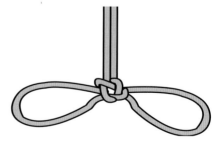

2. Pull ends up and two side bights out. Work knot until it is tight and bights are uniform. Completed Japanese Loop.

58

LANYARD KNOTS

Lanyard knots are used to secure objects to a rope or as a stopper knot. To make lanyard knots, a three or four stranded rope is used.

DIAMOND KNOT

This decorative knot is used to form the eye of a lanyard or the commencement of a bell rope.

2. The blue strand is taken outside the brown and up through the bight of the tan.

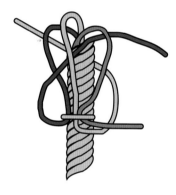

3. The brown strand is taken outside of the tan and up through the bight of the blue.

1. Unravel rope strands and bend them down along the rope.

4. Finally the tan is taken outside the blue and up through the bight of the brown.

59

5. Knot can be repeated, added to, or trimmed. Completed Diamond Knot.

DOUBLE DIAMOND KNOT

This will make a bulkier knot than the Diamond Knot.

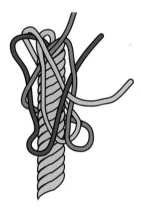

1. Unravel rope strands and bend down along the rope. Follow steps 2-4 of the Diamond Knot (pg 59).

2. Work cord until tight. End of rope can be seized. Completed Double Diamond Knot.

WALL KNOT • PIG-TAIL
• WALNUT KNOT
• WHALE KNOT

The Wall Knot is a stopper at the end of a three strand rope. The ends can be trimmed, frayed, or added to with another knot.

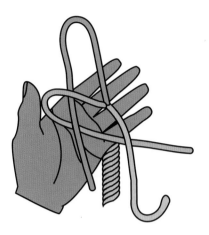

1. Separate rope strands. Pass each strand in turn around and under its neighbor.

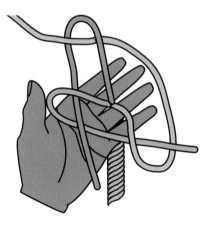

2. Pass the end of the third strand upwards through the bight formed by the first.

3. Pull tight. If made correctly, all three strands emerge from the top of the knot. Completed Wall Knot.

CROWN KNOT

The Crown Knot is the exact opposite of the Wall Knot. If either of these knots are turned upside down it becomes the other knot. The Crown Knot is seldom used unsupported. It normally is the basis to more intricate lanyard knots.

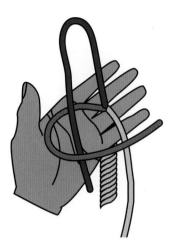

1. Separate rope strands. Form two equal side loops. Holding the loops closed, form a third loop beneath them by moving the end and the standing part upwards in a counterclockwise direction. Still holding base of bight, take right side loop and turn it downwards.

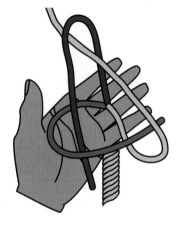

2. Take left side loop over folded right loop and insert through bottom loop.

4. Pull loops to tighten the knot, being certain both loops are equal. Pull tight.

5. Completed Crown Knot.

FOOTROPE KNOT
● KOP KNOT ● MANROPE KNOT ● SKULL PIG-TAIL ● TACK KNOT

The Footrope Knot consists of a Crown Knot tied on a Wall Knot. This knot tends to hold tighter and look more complete.

MATTHEW WALKER

A slight variation of the Wall Knot, is to pass each strand around two neighboring strands instead of one, making a Matthew Walker.

1. Unravel rope strands. Bring each strand through loop of strand to the right.

3. For the third time, bring each strand through loop of strand to the right.

2. Again take each strand through loop of strand to the right.

4. Pull tight. Seize rope end. Completed Matthew Walker.

MATTHEW WALKER FOUR STRAND

This lanyard knot is similar to the Matthew Walker just tied with one more strand.

1. Unravel strands on end of rope.

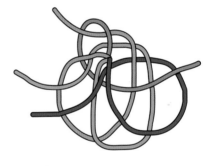

3. Bring end through the loop at the right for a total of four times.

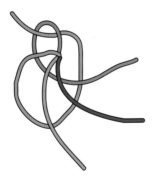

2. Bring each strand through loop of strand to the right.

4. Pull tight. Seize rope end. Completed Matthew Walker Four Strand.

TIE IT SPORTY

Camel Hitch
Farrier's Halter Loop

FISHING

HOOK TIE

This strong attachment is used by fisherman for securing eye hooks and creating a starting point for placing tackle.

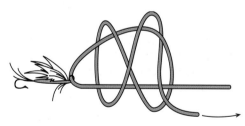

1. Take line through hook. Wrap around standing end in a figure eight shape.

2. Pull end to tighten. Completed Hook Tie.

OVERHAND LOOP
• LOOP FISH KNOT

The Overhand Loop is widely accepted as a simple way to attach hooks and swivels.

1. Double line and thread through eye of hook. Make an Overhand Knot (pg 12). Pull line through loop and slide knot together.

2. Completed Overhand Loop.

BIMINI TWIST

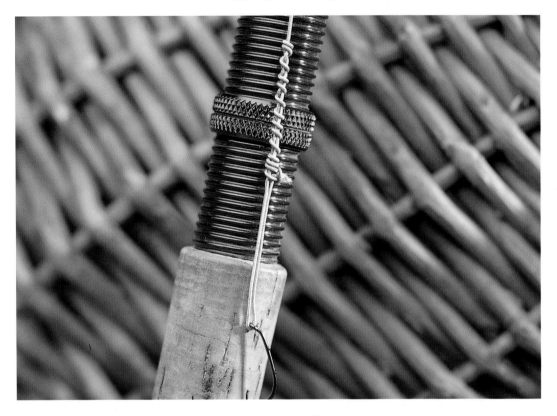

The Bimini Twist is tied in the reel line to attach spinners and lures.

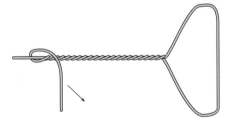

1. Make a bight in the reel line. Twist about 20 wraps. Transfer bight onto feet keeping tension on both sides. Pull ends apart at top.

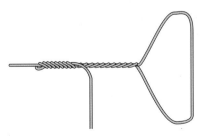

2. Wrap working end downward to create a second layer of turns.

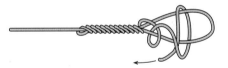

3. Make a couple of Half Hitches (pg 14), the first around one part of the bight, the second around both parts.

4. Completed Bimini Twist.

67

PERFECTION LOOP
• ANGLER'S LOOP

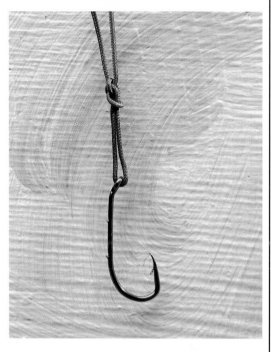

This loop can be tied quickly. It is not suggested for use with rope because of its tendency to jam.

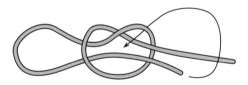

1. Tie an Overhand Knot (pg 12) with a bight. Bring end behind and back through loop.

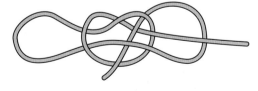

2. Weave end through center loop.

3. Pull tight. Completed Perfection Loop.

BLOOD DROPPER LOOP

This knot creates loops at different intervals along a line to add more flies (called droppers) to the line.

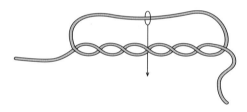

1. Make a triple Overhand Knot (pg 12) with a bight in the middle.

2. Pull the bight down through the center.

3. Pull tight. Completed Blood Dropper Loop.

HALF BLOOD KNOT

This knot is used to attaching hooks to a line.

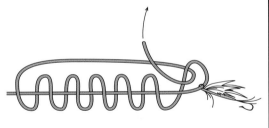

1. Thread hook eye onto line. Wrap working end around standing part 3½ times, coming back through first loop.

2. Wrap around loop and tighten around hook eye. Completed Half Blood Knot.

BLOOD KNOT
• BARREL KNOT

This knot is used to join fine nylon line of the same or similar diameter together.

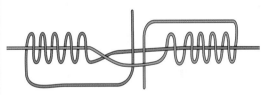

1. Place two ends alongside one another. Take end left and make two turns around other line. Bend left end and insert between two lines at point of intersection. Repeat with right end. The knot is now complete but loose; before pulling tight, check that it is perfectly symmetrical. Draw up by pulling ends and then the standing parts of the two lines.

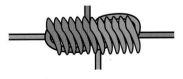

2. Completed Blood Knot.

TURLE KNOT
- MAJOR TURLE'S KNOT
  - THE TURTLE

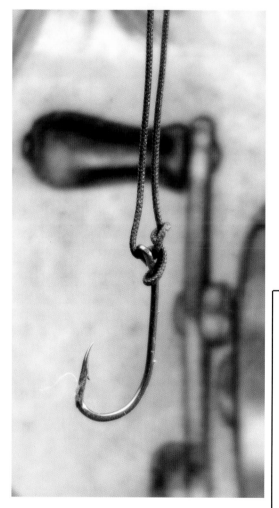

This knot is used to secure gut to a hook.

1. Thread hook onto line. Loop and knot end of line.

70

2. Take hook through loop. Pull knot snugly. Take care loop does not catch on hackles of the fly.

3. Draw knot tight on upper side of hook neck. Completed Turle Knot.

DOUBLE TURLE KNOT

Adding another wrap to a Turle Knot makes the stronger Double Turle Knot.

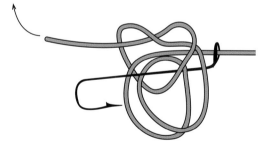

1. Thread hook onto line. Wrap line around hook twice before knotting the end. Complete knot by following steps 2 and 3 of the Turle Knot.

2. Completed Double Turle Knot.

Double Turle Knot

catch of the day

Interlocking Loops are a strong yet simple way to join a hook length of nylon to a reel line. Loops are made using the Bight Loop to secure.

BIGHT LOOP

INTERLOCKING LOOPS

1. Make a bight in line. Fold and twist.

2. Bring bight through loop.

3. Pull tight. Completed Bight Loop.

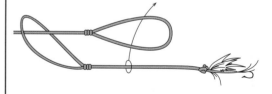

1. Thread one loop through the other.

2. Pull line through loop.

3. Completed Interlocking Loops.

CLINCH KNOT
- MONOFILAMENT FISHING • TUCKED HALF BLOOD

1. Thread line through hook. Twist line and bring end back through loop. Bring end down between twisted line and pulled line. Tighten by pulling standing end of line.

This knot is used to fasten a hook to a leader.

2. Completed Clinch Knot.

HAYWIRE TWIST

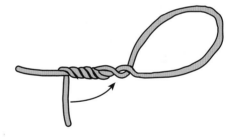

1. Make a bight and twist end around standing part. Bring standing part up through first twist to secure.

2. Completed Haywire Twist.

This knot is used to attach a lure or swivel.

DOUBLE OVERHAND LOOP • OLD WATER LOOP

This knot is used to join plastic cords.

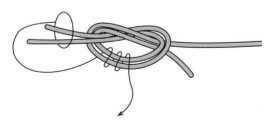

1. Tie an Overhand Knot (pg 12) with both cords together. Wrap ends around bight three times.

2. Tighten by pulling on both ends. Completed Double Overhand Loop.

74

FRENCH KNOT

The French Knot, used in embroidery, is a variation of the Double Overhand Loop. The multiple turns are taken over the needle and pulled through the material.

COMPOUND KNOT

This knot is used to make a loop in the end of a filament or other leader.

1. Make a Slip Knot (pg 12). Pull bight through. Weave end through.

2. Pull tight. Completed Compound Knot.

TRUE LOVER'S KNOT • ANGLER'S KNOT
• ENGLISH KNOT • ENGLISHMAN'S KNOT
• FISHERMAN'S KNOT • HALIBUT KNOT • WATER KNOT

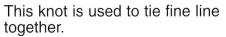

This knot is used to tie fine line together.

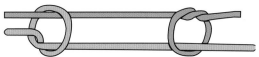

1. Tie two Overhand Knots (pg 12).

2. Slip ends through loops. Pull ends to bring loops together. Completed True Lover's Knot.

CLIMBING

A climber's knot must be strong and secure. Check with a professional for advice on the best knots to use in every climbing situation.

FIGURE EIGHT LOOP
• FIGURE EIGHT ON THE BIGHT • GUIDE KNOT

The Figure Eight Loop is suitable for use with a strain on either or both ends of the rope. It is reliable with stiff or slippery line. It is heavy and bulky and tightening can make it difficult to undo but it is easily and quickly tied.

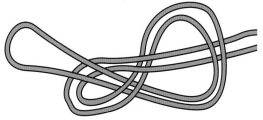

1. Pull out a bight of rope to form a loop and tie in the doubled rope as the Figure Eight Knot (pg 77).

2. Tighten by pulling on the loop. Completed Figure Eight Loop.

PRUSIK KNOT

The Prusik Knot uses a looped thin line and is tied to a heavier rope to use as footholds. When load is released the knot can be moved to a new position.

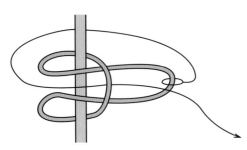

1. Form a Cow Hitch (pg 15) around heavier rope.

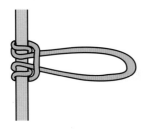

2. Form another Cow Hitch through original loop. Completed Prusik Knot.

76

DOUBLE MUNTER FRICTION HITCH

Used by climbers as a safety line. It is capable of absorbing the energy of a fall. The knot will lock to catch a falling climber.

1. Weave rope twice around link and standing part.

2. Completed Double Munter Friction Hitch.

MUNTER FRICTION HITCH • ITALIAN HITCH
• SLIDING RING HITCH

Used for the same reason as the Double Munter Friction Hitch but needed for larger diameter rope.

1. Weave rope around link and standing part.

2. Completed Munter Friction Hitch.

FIGURE EIGHT BEND
• FLEMISH BEND

This knot joins two slippery ropes.

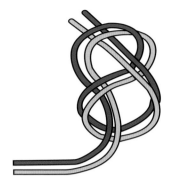

1. With ropes together, bend into a figure eight shape. Bring ends up through top loop.

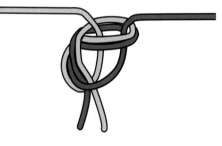

2 Push end down through loop.

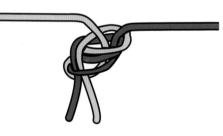

3. Completed Figure Eight Bend.

FIGURE EIGHT KNOT
• FLEMISH KNOT
• LANYARD • SAVOY KNOT

This stopper is the same as the Figure Eight Bend but it is made with one rope in itself.

MAGNUS HITCH
• MAGNER'S HITCH

This hitch attaches a line to a spar or to another line. The knot has a ratchet action which allows it to be slid one way but locks against a pull in the opposite direction. It is easy to secure and easy to cast off.

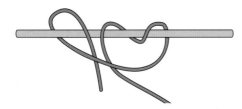

1. Loop rope around spar twice. Take a turn around rope above hitch.

2. Pull ends down and push loops together to tighten. Completed Magnus Hitch.

78

TREE SURGEON'S KNOT • ARBOREAL HITCH

This modification of the Magnus Hitch can be moved up and down by hand, but remains secure when lateral strain is applied.

1. Make a Magnus Hitch. Add an extra turn. Completed Tree Surgeon's Knot.

CAMEL HITCH

The Camel Hitch came out of the need for a knot that was secure but easy to untie when wet.

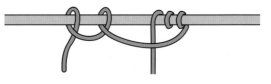

1. Wrap end around post twice. Bring end in front of wraps and make a couple of Half Hitches (pg 14) to the left. Completed Camel Hitch.

ALPINE BUTTERFLY
- BUTTERFLY NOOSE
- LINEMAN LOOP

FIGURE EIGHT NOOSE

The Alpine Butterfly fits around a climber's chest. It can be tied quickly, untied easily, does not slip, and the loop does not shrink when the knot is tightened.

This knot is easy to tie and stays tied, even in stiff rope. It is used to attach a line to a carabiner.

1. Pass rope through center of an Overhand Knot (pg 12).

1. Form figure eight with rope end.

2. Completed Alpine Butterfly.

2. Bring end through loop.

3. Pull tight. Completed Figure Eight Noose.

79

BOWLINE IN A BIGHT

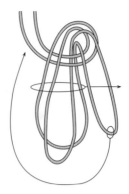

2. Form a loop. Thread bight through loop and bend bight from back over end of loop to restrict widening. Continue bending it back right around loop until it comes up to standing part again.

This reliable knot is used in rescue work. It forms two fixed loops that do not slide and can be used separately.

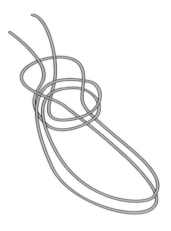

3. Be careful not to confuse the loop and the bight, which has to be pulled tight. The knot is worked by pulling the standing parts and the eye of the loop at the same time.

1. Double end into a bight and overlap standing end into loops.

4. Completed Bowline in a Bight.

ONTARIO BOWLINE | ALGONQUIN BOWLINE

The Ontario Bowline overcomes the weakness in older stiffer climbing ropes.

The Algonquin Bowline, made in worn rope, retains a knot when rope cannot be fully tightened.

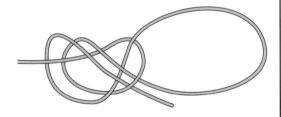

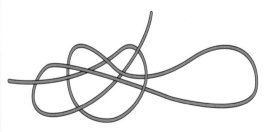

1. Make an Overhand Knot (pg 12). Bring end back around, doubling the overland loop.

1. Make an Overhand Knot (pg 12). Weave end through center.

2. Pull tight. Completed Ontario Bowline.

2. Pull tight. Completed Algonquin Bowline.

81

LIGHTERMAN'S BACK MOORING HITCH
• TUGBOAT HITCH • NO-NAME KNOT

This hitch can hold firmly, yet can be cast free in a few seconds.

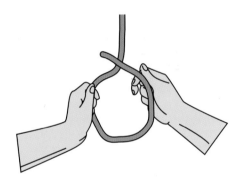

1. Take one or two round turns.

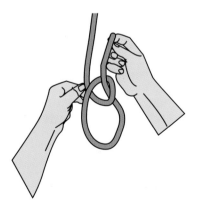

2. Take a bight under and around standing end.

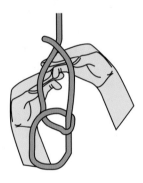

3. Loop it over top and wrap working end around a couple of times.

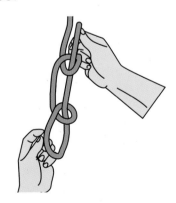

4. Repeat as often as required to prevent slipping under load. Completed Lighterman's Back Mooring Hitch.

BOWLINE • BOLIN KNOT • BOWLING • BULIN KNOT

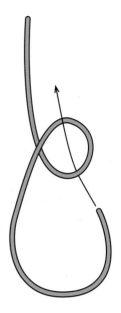

1. Form a loop in standing part of rope. Pass working end up through eye of loop.

The Bowline is probably the most useful knot on a boat. It does not slip, jam, or come loose. It is easy to tie, and untie even after being under heavy strain. It makes a hand-hold for waterskiing, a permanent knot to tie up a boat or to secure tent ropes for staking.

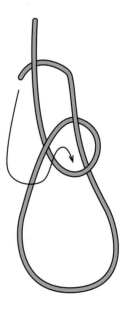

2. Go around back of standing part, and then back down through eye once more.

3. Tighten by holding onto bight and pulling on standing part. Completed Bowline.

DOUBLE BOWLINE
• ROUND TURN BOWLINE

A Double Bowline adds a Half Hitch to a Bowline for extra security when towing over rough terrain or through choppy water.

RUNNING BOWLINE

A Running Bowline is a Bowline tied around its own standing part, forming a noose.

SLIPPED BOWLINE

The Slipped Bowline adds a bight for the final tuck of a Bowline. This makes the knot easier to untie when under great strain.

STANDING BOWLINE

A Standing Bowline is a Bowline with the end seized for greater security.

Bowline Hitch
Fisherman's Bend

84

BOWLINE HITCH

This hitch secures boats at the dock. If it is attached to an anchor ring, a stopper knot should be added for safety.

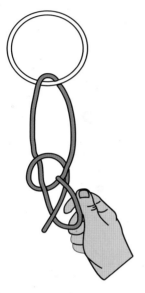

1. Tie an Overhand Knot (pg 12). Pass end behind standing part and insert end into loop.

2. Pull standing part to tighten. Completed Bowline Hitch.

FISHERMAN'S BEND
• ANCHOR HITCH

This is one of the most secure and widely used hitches. It is normally made in thin rope.

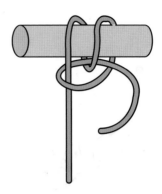

1. Pass end around object two or three times. Pass end behind standing part and insert through turns around object.

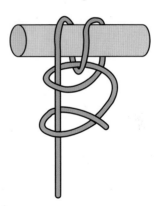

2. Make two or three Half Hitches (pg 14) to secure.

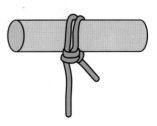

3. Pull tight. Completed Fisherman's Bend.

PILE HITCH

This quick and easy hitch works best with medium to heavy line. It is used for securing objects to a post or mooring a boat.

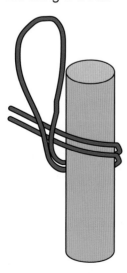

1. Loop doubled rope around object. Bring looped end up over standing end.

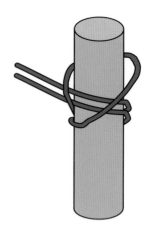

2. Place loop over object and pull to secure. Completed Pile Hitch.

HORSES

DOUBLE HORSE NOOSE

The Double Horse Noose is a variation of the Pile Hitch but is used around the neck and nose of a horse.

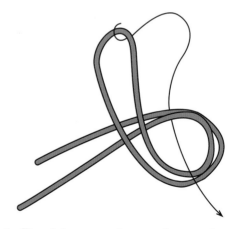

1. Double rope in center and bring through bight.

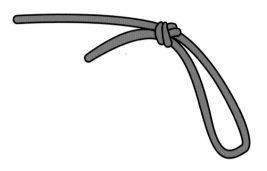

2. Make loop desired size. Pull knot tight.

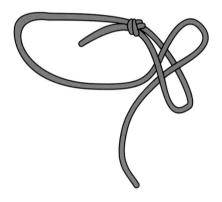

3. Form a bight in standing end of rope. Pass bight through loop.

4. Position on horse. Completed Double Horse Noose.

HARNESS LOOP
- ARTILLERY LOOP
- ARTILLERYMAN'S HITCH
- BUTTERFLY KNOT
- HARNESS HITCH
- MAN-HARNESS HITCH

This loop forms a bight which tolerates tension from both sides. This is a hauling loop to put in a rope without using the ends.

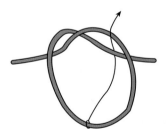

1. Make an Overhand Knot (pg 12). Weave bottom of loop through. Pull tight.

2. Completed Harness Loop.

DOUBLE HARNESS LOOP

This variation of the Harness Loop adds an extra turn for more security.

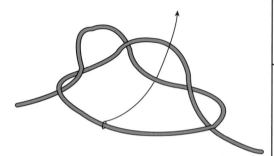

1. Make an Overhand Knot (pg 12). Weave bottom through.

2. Pull tight. Completed Double Harness Loop.

LINEMAN'S LOOP
• MIDDLEMAN'S LOOP

The Lineman's Loop is more secure than the Harness Loop.

1. Make two loops side by side. Weave bottom of loops through center.

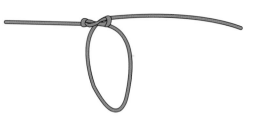

2. Pull loops tight. Completed Lineman's Loop.

FISHERMAN'S LOOP

The Fisherman's Loop is the same as the Lineman's Loop but the ends are used.

FARMER'S HALTER LOOP • DEPARTMENT-STORE LOOP

The Farmer's Halter Loop allows an animal to be led without the loop slipping and choking the animal.

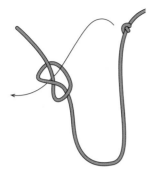

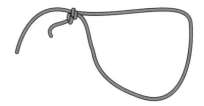

2. Pull to tighten, bringing knots together. Completed Farmer's Halter Loop.

1. Make an Overhand Knot (pg 12) in end of rope. Make an Overhand Knot in standing part. Bring end through Overhand Knot.

HALTER HITCH • HITCHING TIE • MANGER TIE • SLIP NOOSE HITCH

The Halter Hitch is used to secure animals to a post. It is easy to release.

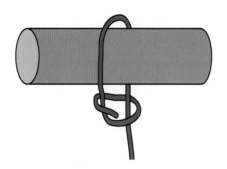

1. Loop rope over post. Make an Overhand Knot (pg 12) in end of rope and bring end through.

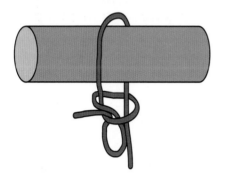

2. Make a bight through the loop.

3. Bring end back down through bight.

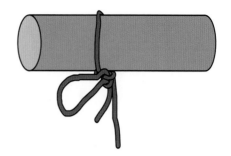

4. Completed Halter Hitch.

NOOSE HITCH
• FARMER'S HITCH

This variation of the Halter Hitch does not include a slip causing the hitch to jam and making it difficult to untie.

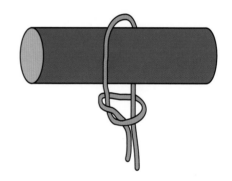

1. Loop rope over post. Make an Overhand Knot (pg 12) over the standing part.

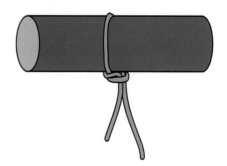

2. Completed Noose Hitch.

HIGHWAYMAN'S
HITCH • DRAW HITCH

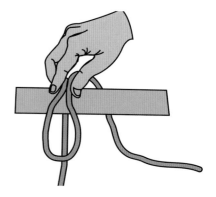

1. Make a bight by folding back a long end and bend it over post. Reaching through this loop, pull up the standing part in a bight.

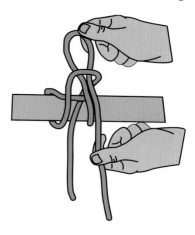

2. Pull tight. Hold the bight secure with the right hand, form another loop with the left hand.

This hitch is useful for tethering animals, lowering loads, and as a temporary fastening. Named from legends of highwaymen and robbers who needed a quick release of their horses reins to ensure a fast getaway.

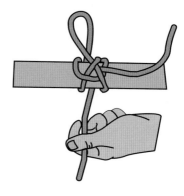

3. Pass new loop through previous loop. Completed Highwayman's Hitch. Pull standing part to tighten. To untie, pull end.

TIMBER HITCH

- COUNTRYMAN'S KNOT
- LUMBERMAN'S KNOT

The Timber Hitch tightens to grip a rough surface like a tree or log.

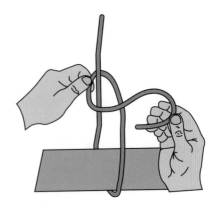

1. Take end around tree then around standing part. Twist it back on itself.

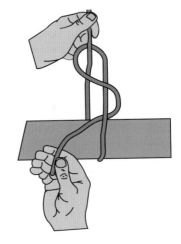

2. Turn three or four times back on itself.

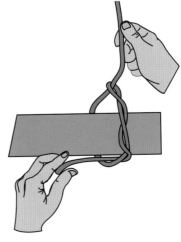

3. Pull tight. Completed Timber Hitch.

BACKWALL HITCH
• BLACKWALL

Using a large-diameter rope; this simple attachment to a hook is used for hoisting light objects.

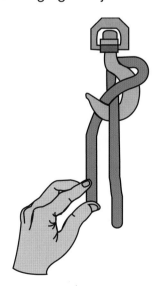

1. Pass rope forward through mouth of hook. Completed Backwall Hitch.

MIDSHIPMAN'S HITCH
• BILL HITCH

This hitch is a continuation of the Backwall Hitch; used to hoist objects with a hook.

1. Make a Backwall Hitch. Wind end around hook; forming a simple knot.

2. Pull standing part and knot will set itself tight. Completed Midshipman's Hitch.

93

AFRICAN RAFTER LASHING

This hitch is used to lash poles together at a right angle.

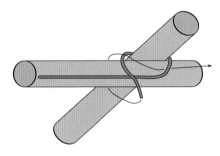

1. Weave rope around pole in a figure eight fashion.

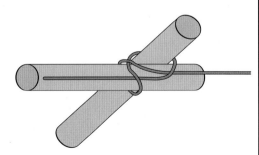

2. Bring end under loop. Pull tight. Completed African Rafter Lashing.

BUOY ROPE HITCH

This hitch is used to lash poles together vertically.

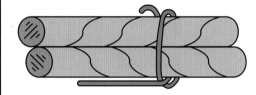

1. Wrap rope around object three times from left to right.

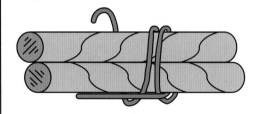

2. Catch standing part with each turn.

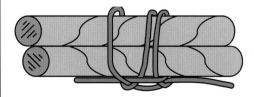

3. Bring working end over last two turns and under first. Seize ends. Completed Buoy Rope Hitch.

Lobster Buoy Hitch
Forked Loop

LOBSTER BUOY HITCH

The Lobster Buoy Hitch is used for hitching to timber.

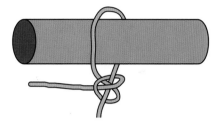

1. Bring working end over object. Take end around standing end and through loop. Take end around standing part again and through newly made loop. Tighten next to object.

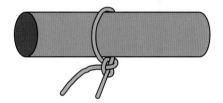

2. Completed Lobster Buoy Hitch.

FORKED LOOP

The Forked Loop acts as a sling for objects such as a horizontal ladder where the loops are each put over one side.

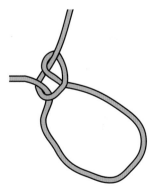

1. Make a loose Overhand Knot (pg 12) far enough back from end to allow for two loops.

95

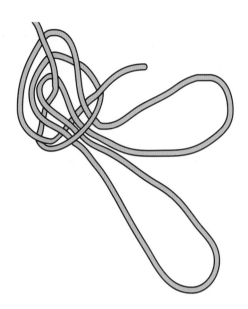

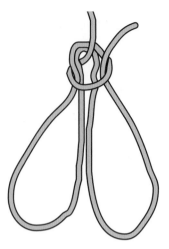

3. Pull knot tight. Take end around standing part. Either tuck end under itself or make an Overhand Knot (pg 12).The knot finishes with the loops on opposite sides. Completed Forked Loop.

2. Pass a bight of the end back through the knot and adjust the resulting two loops to the desired sizes.

POULIE

This French pulley knot is used by campers and woodsmen to stretch strongly or hold something in position, or to haul heavy objects with a stout rope.

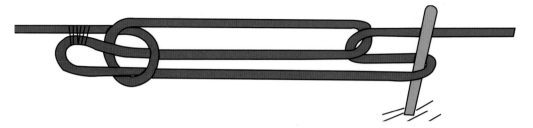

1. Make a loop. Make a bight two feet or more away from the loop. Make a second bight and pass it through the loop. Seize loop to end. Pass standing end of rope around a stout stake, driven firmly into the ground, and up through the first (upper) bight. Completed Poulie.

TENDEUR

This pulley-type knot is used by campers instead of slides for tightening tent guy ropes.

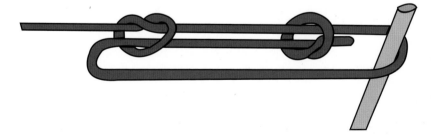

1. Make an Overhand Knot (pg 12) two or three feet from the end of the guy line. The end of the rope is then brought around the tent peg and through the Overhand Knot. Another Overhand Knot is made over the standing part, at end of rope. Completed Tendeur.

TIE IT USEFUL

Slipped Half Hitch
Fire Hose Hitch

CARRICK BEND • ANCHOR BEND • COWBOY KNOT • JOSEPHINE KNOT • SAILOR'S KNOT • SPLIT KNOT • WAKE KNOT • WARP KNOT

This is a Josephine Knot in macrame, Split Knot to knitters, Warp Knot to sailors, Cowboy Knot to cowboys; a knot for everyone. The Carrick Bend is used for absolute security under heavy loads but requires skill and practice to tie.

2. Travel counterclockwise over upper standing part, under upper end.

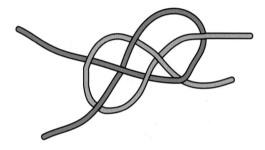

3. Go over upper loop, under standing part of lower line, and over remaining leg of upper loop.

4. Leave ends of both lines long; loading causes a Carrick Bend to capsize into a more compact and stable form. Completed Carrick Bend.

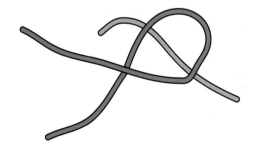

1. Form a loop with first rope. Bring second line under open loop of first.

99

REEVING LINE BEND

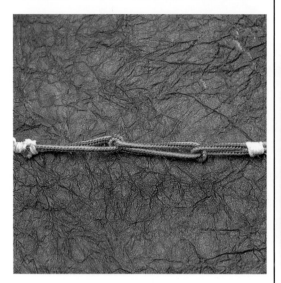

This compact knot is useful when bending lines which must pass through small hawser pipes or a small towing chock, where bigger bends jam.

1. Make a loop in end of rope. Pass rope through loop.

2. Make a loop in new line until it encircles first.

3. Seize ends to secure bend. Completed Reeving Line Bend.

100

HEAVING LINE BEND

The Heaving Line Bend is used to attach a lighter line to a heavy rope for heaving.

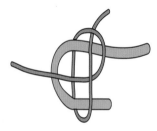

1. Make a bight in the heavier rope. Pass the end of the smaller rope through the bight and weave it around the larger rope.

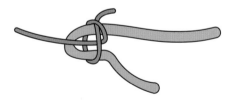

2. Completed Heaving Line Bend.

RACKING BEND

This bend is similar to the Heaving Line Bend but the turns continue around the heavier rope drawing the sides of the thin line together.

ORDINARY KNOT

This knot is similar to the True Lover's Loop (pg 42) but secures two lines together instead of looping in one line.

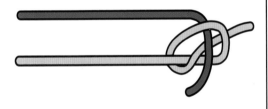

1. Take one rope and tie a loose Overhand Knot (pg 12) near one end. Take the other rope and bring it through the knot.

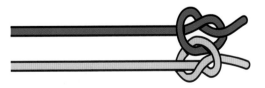

2. Tie the second rope into an Overhand Knot. Pull the two knots tightly at the same time. Completed Ordinary Knot.

GRASS BEND

A Grass Bend joins flat, semi-flexible materials, such as straps, grass, and webbing.

1. Loop each end around other strap. Pull tight. Completed Grass Bend.

BINDER TWINE BEND

Farmers frequently use this knot for joining twine which must pass through binder machinery.

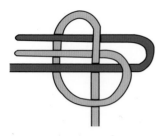

1. Make an Overhand Knot (pg 12) with one length of twine. Weave the other length of twine through loops. Pull tight.

2. Completed Binder Twine Bend.

HUNTER'S BEND
● RIGGER'S BEND

The Hunter's Bend is easy to tie, secure, strong, and holds line well.

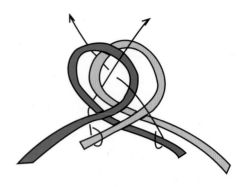

1. Loop both ropes next to each other. Bring an end of each through center.

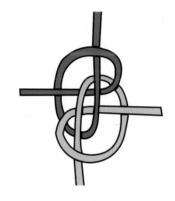

2. The ropes are intertwined as Overhand Knots (pg 12).

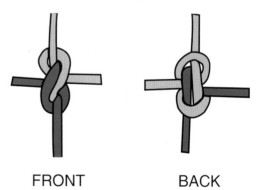

FRONT   BACK

3. Pull the two ends, which protrude laterally from their respective knots. Pull standing parts to tighten knot fully. Completed Hunter's Bend.

Studding-Sail Bend

The following halyard bends are used to attach to an anchor or a spar. They differ in the number of turns or the method of tucking the end.

GAFF TOPSAIL HALYARD BEND

This neat, snug hitch is easily untied. The end should be nipped well up on top of the spar.

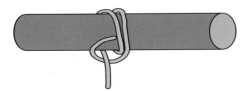

1. Wrap end around object. Bring end around standing part and through loops. Completed Gaff Topsail Halyard Bend.

STUDDING-SAIL BEND

This bend adds a tuck to a Gaff Topsail Halyard Bend.

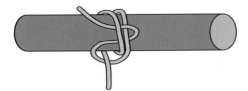

1. Make a Gaff Topsail Halyard Bend. Weave end through rope. Completed Studding-Sail Bend.

TOPSAIL HALYARD BEND

The added turn in the Topsail Halyard Bend makes a sturdier bend than the Studding-Sail Bend.

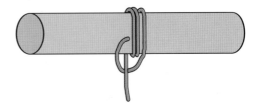

1. Make a Studding-Sail Bend with an extra turn.

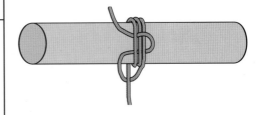

2. Completed Topsail Halyard Bend.

HITCHES

WELL PIPE HITCH
• LIFTING HITCH

The Well Pipe Hitch is used to hoist cylindrical objects such as pipes and poles.

1. Make several turns around pipe from top to bottom.

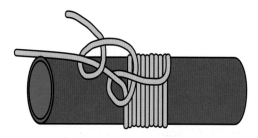

2. Make two Half Hitches (pg 14) around standing part. Completed Well Pipe Hitch.

FIRE HOSE HITCH

The Fire Hose Hitch is used to hoist hose vertically.

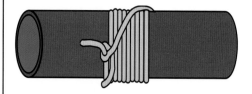

1. Wrap turns around pipe. Bring end back over wraps. Make a Half Hitch (pg 14) around standing part. Completed Fire Hose Hitch.

TRUCKER'S HITCH • POWER-CINCH
• WAGONER'S HITCH

The Trucker's Hitch is a combination of knots put together to get some leverage when tightening. This hitch is good for cinching down a load.

1. Make a loop near end of rope.

3. Run end through hook, bumper, or other object.

2. Make a bight in standing end of rope. Push through loop.

4. Run end through loop. Completed Trucker's Hitch.

RACKING HITCH

This hitch is a Trucker's Hitch with the loops going counterclockwise.

TEAMSTER'S HITCH

The Teamster's Hitch is used to tie a load to a truck or wagon. If the truck is fitted with hooks, the Cow Hitch (pg 15) is tied using the hooks and the load is tightened with the final knot.

1. Tie a long Cow Hitch (pg 15) over a ring or hook.

3. Wrap end in opposite direction.

2. Wrap end around standing part twice.

4. Bring end through first loops. Pull tight. Completed Teamster's Hitch.

PICKET-LINE HITCH
- ARTILLERYMAN'S PICKET
- FISHERMAN'S GROUND LINE HITCH
- SACK KNOT

Since the ends of the Picket-Line Hitch are secured under a turn this hitch will not slip.

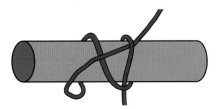

1. Wrap rope around object. Wrap again crossing first wrap. Weave end through loops.

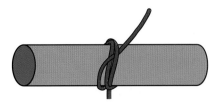

2. Completed Picket-Line Hitch.

CROSSING LINE HITCH

This hitch is used in line formations by taking a distance then forming another hitch.

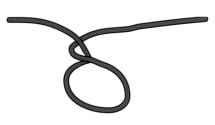

1. Carry rope end around object and across standing part, then exert opposite pressure so that one portion of the rope draws upon the other.

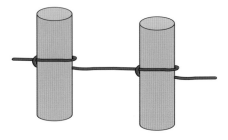

2. Place stakes in desired line. Twist a bight in rope and drop over each stake. Completed Crossing Line Hitches.

SCAFFOLD PLANK HITCH • STAGE HITCH

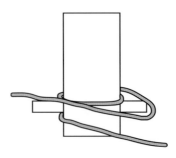

2. The first turn is then not only lifted over the second, but its bight is also passed around the long end of the horn, resulting in two parts of rope crossing the underside of the horn diagonally.

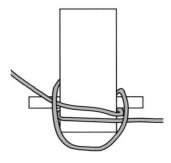

3. The original second turn is then lifted completely over the first and third turns and this bight placed downward over the end of the stage.

This hitch is made at both ends of a plank of wood to support the plank, or stage when used as a scaffold.

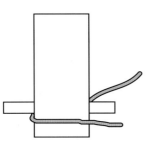

1. Take a turn on inside of horn and a turn on the outside. The rope should cross the horn on the underside.

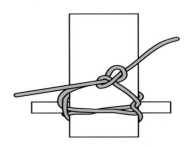

4. Pull to tighten around horn. Make a Bowline (pg 83-84) some distance above the stage. Completed Scaffold Plank Hitch.

KILLICK HITCH • KILLEG HITCH • SLINGSTONE HITCH

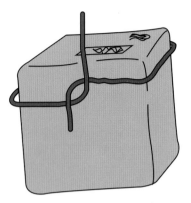

1. Wrap rope around object. Make a turn over standing part.

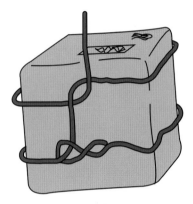

2. Make another turn in the opposite direction and loop it over the bight formed.

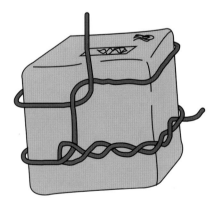

The Killick Hitch is named for a block of stone used as an anchor for a small boat. Since it is used in water, the rope tends to swell, making a permanent fastening.

3. Turn rope around itself several times. Pull tight. Completed Killick Hitch.

HAMMOCK HITCH

Though the Hammock Hitch is not effective in heavy rope, the grip works well for small stuff.

2. Add a Half Hitch (pg 14).

3. Add another Half Hitch.

4. Pull tight. Completed Hammock Hitch.

1. Loop rope through ring. Make an Overhand Knot (pg 12).

STRAP KNOT
- ### LEATHER STRAP HITCH

The Strap Knot is made in leather or webbing to secure two straps.

1. Make a slit in one strap. Bring other strap through slit.

2. Bring strap around and underneath itself. Pull tight. Completed Strap Knot.

DOUBLE RING

Like the Strap Knot, the Double Ring's security is never in question because it has no ends. The knot is used by lobster men to surround their pots.

1. Make a bight in center of rope. Bring ends through bight. Bring ends back through center of newly formed loop.

2. Pull tight.

3. Completed Double Ring.

CAT'S PAW • HOOK HITCH • STROB HITCH

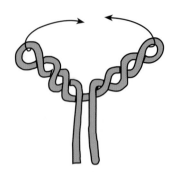

1. Form two loops. Twist three or four times under equal tension, one side going clockwise, the other counterclockwise.

This hitch is used for lifting or towing heavy loads. If one leg should break, the other will hold enough for the load to be lowered safely to the ground.

2. Pass both loops over hook. Tighten by pulling standing parts. Completed Cat's Paw.

BALE SLING

This hitch is used to sling a load from a crane hook with a strop.

1. Make a bight in a circled rope. Take bight through other end of rope placing barrel in center. Completed Bale Sling.

ROPE LADDER

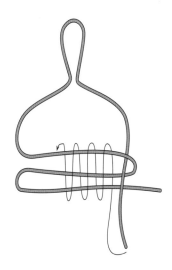

1. Form an "S" with one side of rope. Wrap rope around bight.

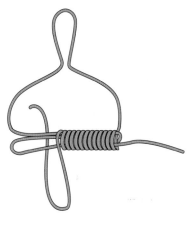

2. Pull rope through last loop. Alternate sides after each rung.

The Rope Ladder can be made with twin tails or doubled in half with an eye in the rope bight.

3. Weave other side of rope through and around. Ladder width should be about a foot. Completed Rope Ladder.

TOM FOOL'S KNOT

This knot is used for emergency handcuffs or as a sling for a jar.

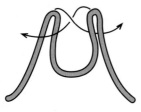

1. Make two bights in rope. Cross one loop over other.

2. Pull loops through. Pull tight.

3. Completed Tom Fool's Knot.

HANDCUFF
• DOUBLE NOOSE

Similar to the Tom Fool's Knot the Handcuff was historically used as a handcuff tie. This noose is now commonly used as a bottle sling. The greater the load, the tighter the grip.

1. Make two overlapping loops. Pull centers through to outside.

2. Pull loops through and tighten.

3. Completed Handcuff.

CHAIR KNOT • FIREMAN'S KNOT • HITCHED TOM FOOL'S KNOT • MAN-HARNESS FROM TOM FOOL'S KNOT

The Chair Knot is used by rescue workers to lift and lower people from high places. The knot is made in the center of a rope which must be at least twice as long as the descent. Slip one loop under armpits and the other under knees. Adjust loops and lock in place. Remember unconscious people can slip through loops.

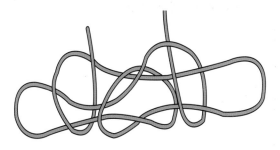

1. Make a Handcuff (pg 114). Make a loop around each bight.

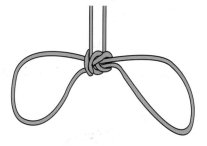

2. Pull loops to tighten knot. Completed Chair Knot.

ENGLISHMAN'S LOOP • COVE KNOT
• MIDDLEMAN'S KNOT • OVERHAND BEND
• WATERMAN'S KNOT

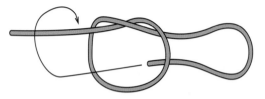

1. Make an Overhand Knot (pg 12). Bring end back through knot.

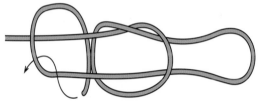

2. Make an Overhand Knot (pg 12) over the standing part.

3. Position two Overhand Knots together.

4. Pull tight until knots are pushed together. Completed Englishman's Loop.

The Englishman's Loop is a good strong loop, however, the knot it produces is quite cumbersome.

SISTER LOOPS

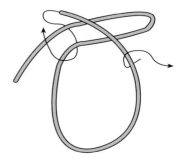

1. Make a bight at end of rope. Loop other end around bight.

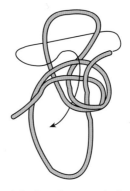

2. Bring bight through loop. With standing end, circle bight.

3. Work loops and knot to make loops even. Pull knot tight. Completed Sister Loops.

The Sister Loops make two identical loops which are used to suspend a load off the ground.

SHORTENING

SHEEPSHANK

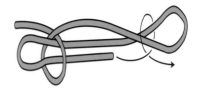

1. Take a bight near rope center. Take another bight in opposite direction, one running upward, the other downward.

2. Make a loop and slip it over upward bight, pulling loop tight. Repeat with downward bight, but in reverse fashion.

3. Completed Sheepshank.

SHEEPSHANK BOWKNOT

When the rope is not damaged but still needs to be shortened a small amount, the ends can be pulled into this knot to secure.

1. Make a Sheepshank. Pull the parts of the knot together snug. Completed Sheepshank Bowknot.

The Sheepshank is used to shorten rope without cutting it or to make a weak spot stronger when it is necessary that the rope be used. This knot will only work when there is even strain on both ends, otherwise it comes loose.

SHEEPSHANK WITH MARLINGSPIKE HITCHES

The Sheepshank with Marlingspike Hitches is the safest of the Sheepshank knots. All other varieties should be seized or otherwise secured to make them safe.

1. Form rope into a backwards "S" shape.

2. Loop each end of rope.

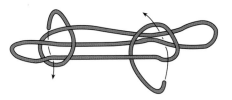

3. Loop around bights and weave through center.

4. Tighten. Completed Sheepshank with Marlingspike Hitches.

Navy Sheepshank

SWORD KNOT
• SHEEPSHANK WITH AN OVERHAND KNOT

The Sword Knot not fully tightened is a trick knot. Pulled tightly or with Half Hitches added, this knot is an effective sheepshank knot.

1. Make four loops. Pull through opposite sides on knot.

2. Completed Sword Knot. Knot will look bunchy and unattractive. Grasp ends of cord and give a strong jerk. Knot will disappear.

NAVY SHEEPSHANK • HANDCUFF KNOT
• MAN-O'-WAR SHEEPSHANK
• SHEEPSHANK WITH A SWORD KNOT

Called many names, this sheepshank is a Sword Knot pulled tight. Half Hitches can be added to each end for security.

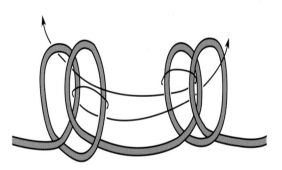

1. Make four loops which overlap each other in pairs. Pull each pair through center of opposite pair.

2. Tightly pull together. Jerk loops a few times to make them tighter. Completed Navy Sheepshank.

LOOP KNOT

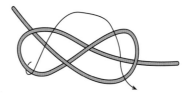

1. Make a bight in the rope with the worn area in the center.

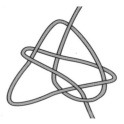

2. Tie an Overhand Knot (pg 12).

This simple and effective knot is used to eliminate a worn section of rope. Commonly used to shorten tow ropes on trucks and cars.

3. Pull tight. Completed Loop Knot.

BOWLINE SHORTENING

This Bowline knot is used when rope is a little longer than needed.

2. Pull ends tight. Completed Bowline Shortening.

1. Make two loops. Cross loops in an Overhand Knot (pg 12).

SHORT SPLICE • OVER-AND-UNDER SPLICE
• REGULAR SPLICE • SAILOR'S SHORT SPLICE

This splice joins two ropes which do not have to run through a pulley of the correct size or through an opening which is only slightly larger than the rope.

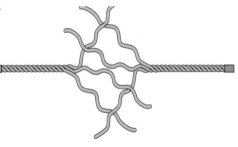

1. Untwist strands a half dozen times. Intertwine alternating strands together. To keep the non-working strands temporarily out of the way lightly whip or tape them.

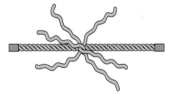

2. Tuck ends under, alternating on one side of splice then the other, until each strand has been tucked under at least three times.

3. Cut off strand ends not too close to rope. When splicing is done, roll and pound on a hard surface with a mallet or back of an ax blade. Completed Short Splice.

SPANISH WINDLASS • WINDLASS CONSTRICTOR • TOURNIQUET

This knot pulls objects together with the twisting rope. Use strong rope, as there can be considerable stretching and frictional strain.

1. Join ends of rope to make an endless loop - a Sheet Bend (pg 22) could be used. The loop must be long enough to go around the load, with some to spare for a lever to be inserted. Twist rope until desired tightness. To hold position, tie the end of the lever to the rope. Completed Spanish Windlass.

INDEX

127